# A Dome
## Stays Strong

Crystal Sikkens
Crabtree Publishing Company
www.crabtreebooks.com

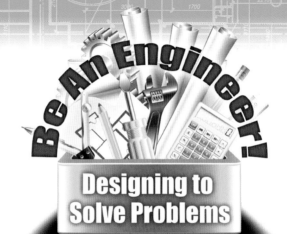

**Be An Engineer!**

## Designing to Solve Problems

**Author:** Crystal Sikkens

**Series research and development:**
Janine Deschenes and Reagan Miller

**Editorial director:** Kathy Middleton

**Editor:** Petrice Custance

**Proofreader:** Kathy Middleton

**Design and photo research:** Katherine Berti

**Print and production coordinator:** Katherine Berti

**Images:**

Alamy: M&N: p. 18

Getty Images: Bettmann: p. 19

Shutterstock
fitzcrittle: p. 17 top
Frank Romeo: p. 17 bottom
Robert Noel de Tilly: p. 12

Wikimedia Commons
Levent Demirörs: p. 22
Mmry0241: p. 13 bottom right

All other images by Shutterstock

**Library and Archives Canada Cataloguing in Publication**

Sikkens, Crystal, author
        A dome stays strong / Crystal Sikkens.

(Be an engineer! Designing to solve problems)
Includes index.
Issued in print and electronic formats.
ISBN 978-0-7787-5159-5 (hardcover).--
ISBN 978-0-7787-5163-2 (softcover).--
ISBN 978-1-4271-2107-3 (HTML)

        1. Domes--Design and construction--Juvenile literature.
2. Domes--Juvenile literature.  3. Structural engineering--Juvenile
literature.  I. Title.

TA660.D6S55 2018          j690'.146          C2018-902991-9
                                             C2018-902992-7

**Library of Congress Cataloging-in-Publication Data**

Names: Sikkens, Crystal, author.
Title: A dome stays strong / Crystal Sikkens.
Description: New York, New York : Crabtree Publishing Company,
  [2019] | Series: Be an engineer! Designing to solve problems |
  Includes index.
Identifiers: LCCN 2018027892 (print) | LCCN 2018029847 (ebook) |
  ISBN 9781427121073 (Electronic) |
  ISBN 9780778751595 (hardcover : alk. paper) |
  ISBN 9780778751632 (pbk. : alk. paper)
Subjects:  LCSH: Domes--Juvenile literature.
Classification: LCC TH2170 (ebook) | LCC TH2170 .S55 2019 (print) |
  DDC  624.1/775--dc23
LC record available at https://lccn.loc.gov/2018027892

## Crabtree Publishing Company

www.crabtreebooks.com      1-800-387-7650

Printed in the U.S.A./092018/CG20180719

**Published in Canada**
**Crabtree Publishing**
616 Welland Ave.
St. Catharines, Ontario
L2M 5V6

**Published in the United States**
**Crabtree Publishing**
PMB 59051
350 Fifth Avenue, 59th Floor
New York, New York 10118

**Published in the United Kingdom**
**Crabtree Publishing**
Maritime House
Basin Road North, Hove
BN41 1WR

**Published in Australia**
**Crabtree Publishing**
3 Charles Street
Coburg North
VIC 3058

# Contents

Hi, I'm Ava and this is Finn. Get ready for an inside look at the world of engineering! The Be an Engineer! series explores how engineers build structures to solve problems.

After reading this book, join us online at Crabtree Plus to help us solve real-world engineering challenges! Just use the Digital Code on page 23 in this book.

# Finding a Solution

Nolan and his family grow vegetables in their backyard to donate to people in need. Unfortunately, the greenhouse they grow the food in has collapsed from snow and strong winds. Nolan wonders if there is a way to stop this from happening again.

# Durable Domes

"What if we built a fence to help block the wind, or put poles inside to hold up the roof?" he thought. Then Nolan remembers reading about domes at school. Maybe he could replace their greenhouse with a geodesic dome. A geodesic dome is a round structure. Its **frame** is made up of triangle shapes.

*Geodesic domes are the strongest type of structure. They get their strength from their shape and by being built with triangles. They can withstand forceful winds, heavy snow, and even **earthquakes**.*

### Did you know?

Geodesic domes can be used for sports stadiums, greenhouses, homes, and other buildings and shelters. They are light and can be set up quickly and easily. They are usually inexpensive to build.

# What Is an Engineer?

Nolan is a problem solver. He enjoys finding solutions to problems, just like an engineer. An engineer is a person who uses math, science, and creative thinking to design things that solve problems and meet needs.

# More Than One Kind

An engineer can put his or her problem-solving skills to use in a number of jobs. For example, some engineers find ways to improve our **environment** or health care. Others develop new products, such as computer software, foods, or structures.

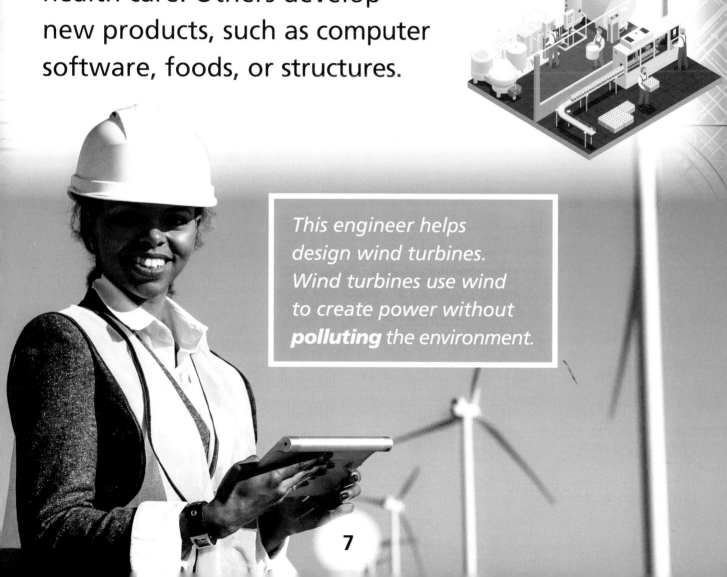

*This engineer helps design wind turbines. Wind turbines use wind to create power without **polluting** the environment.*

# Problem-Solving Steps

An engineer's goal is to find the best solution to a problem. To do this, all engineers follow a set of steps called the Engineering Design Process. They may need to repeat these steps over and over until they find a solution that is both safe and **effective**.

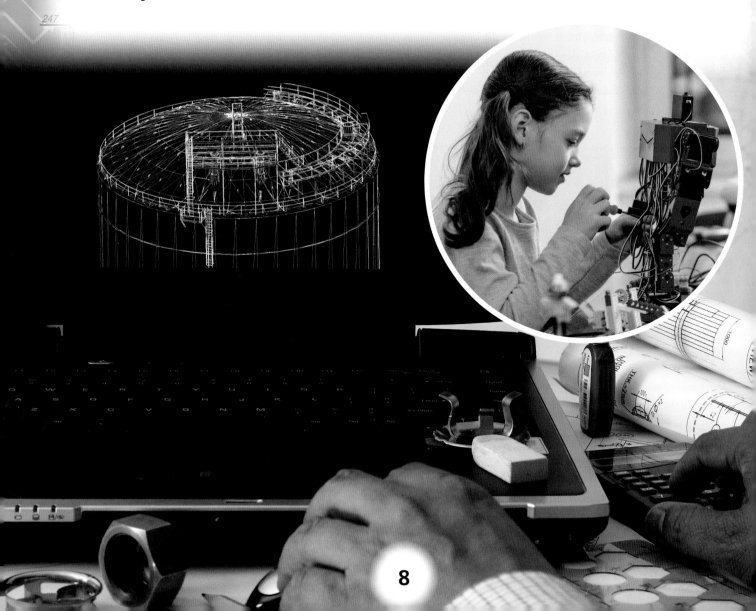

## ASK

Ask questions and gather information about the problem you are trying to solve.

## BRAINSTORM

Work with a group to come up with different ideas to solve the problem. Choose the best solution.

# The Engineering Design Process

## COMMUNICATE

Share your design with others.

## PLAN AND MAKE A MODEL

Create a plan to carry out your solution. Draw a diagram and gather materials. Make a **model** of your solution.

## TEST AND IMPROVE

Test your model and record the results. Using the results, improve, or make your design better. Retest your improved design.

# Asking Questions

The first step in the Engineering Design Process involves asking questions and gathering information. To prevent a greenhouse from collapsing again, an engineer would study the usual weather in the area. They would need to know whether **hurricanes** or **tornadoes** are common, and whether the area tends to get a lot of snow.

*An engineer might need to know what the shape of the greenhouse is and what materials were used to build it.*

# Brainstorming

The second step in the Engineering Design Process is to brainstorm, or discuss possible solutions to the problem with others. Using a web diagram, like the one below, can be helpful for organizing ideas.

**Problem**

How can we prevent wind and snow from collapsing the greenhouse again?

Build a new greenhouse in the shape of a geodesic dome.

Repair any holes in the frame that weaken the structure.

Seal the doors and windows tight so wind cannot get through.

Place poles inside the greenhouse to give extra support to the roof.

Open part of the roof to let snow inside so it won't build up on the roof.

# Designing a Plan

If a geodesic dome is chosen as the best solution, the engineer plans the design. He or she must decide how big it has to be, what features are needed, how it will be attached to the ground, and what building materials to use. The materials depend on what the structure is being used for.

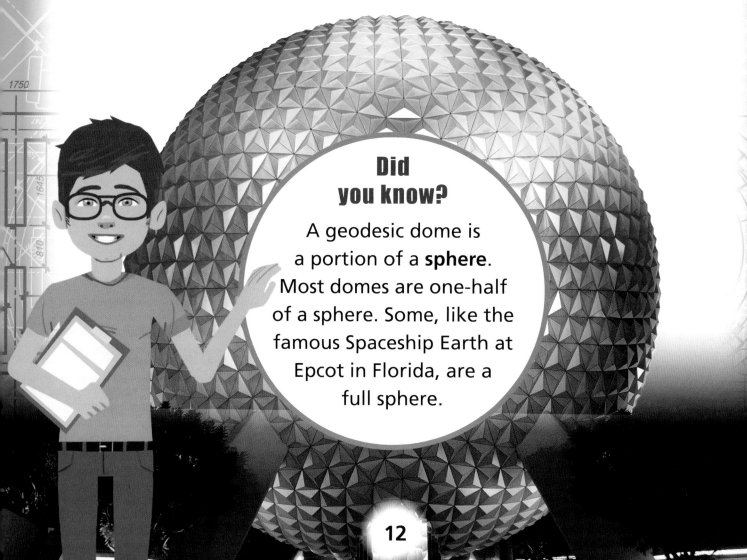

## Did you know?

A geodesic dome is a portion of a **sphere**. Most domes are one-half of a sphere. Some, like the famous Spaceship Earth at Epcot in Florida, are a full sphere.

Some domes are very light. Their plastic or steel frames are covered with only a sturdy sheet of plastic. This makes them ideal for small shelters that are temporary or need to be moved around.

Homes built in the shape of a dome often have a wooden frame, covered with **plywood**. A roof covering, called **shingles**, is usually attached to the plywood to keep out water.

Many large, permanent domes such as stadiums and arenas are built with a steel or aluminum frame. They are covered with concrete, metal, or thick, clear plastic panels.

# Making a Model

Once the planning step is complete, the engineer will create a model of his or her design. A model is a **representation** of a real object. The engineer can use the model to show builders what the dome will look like when it is finished, and how to construct it.

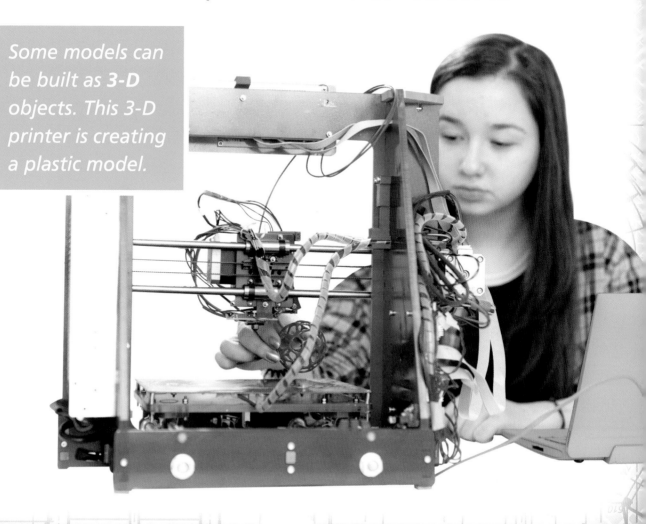

*Some models can be built as **3-D** objects. This 3-D printer is creating a plastic model.*

# Testing and Improving

Engineers also use models to test their design. By testing a model before a dome is built, engineers can see if the materials they selected are the best choice for the dome's purpose. They can also test the dome's strength against wind and weather. After the tests are done, the engineer records the results, makes improvements, and retests.

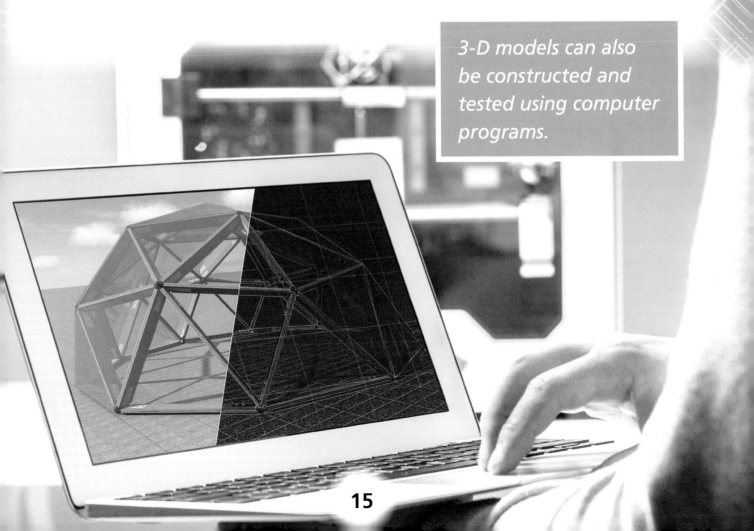

3-D models can also be constructed and tested using computer programs.

# Sharing the Results

The final step in the Engineering Design Process is for the engineers to share their results. Communicating and sharing information helps other engineers find out what worked and what didn't when designing a geodesic dome. This helps engineers build better and safer domes in the future.

> *One popular feature added to many dome sports stadiums today is a **retractable** roof. The roof can be opened in nice weather and closed in cold or rainy weather.*

## Making Improvements

The geodesic dome became popular after American engineer R. Buckminster Fuller began designing them in the 1950s. The basic design of a geodesic dome hasn't changed much since then. However, there have been many improvements in building materials and the features added to them.

# Design Failure

The famous U.S. **pavilion** at the 1967 World Expo in Montreal, Canada, was a giant geodesic dome built by Buckminster Fuller. Unfortunately, Fuller did not consider Canada's dramatic changes in weather in his design. The materials he chose for the dome grew and shrank slightly with the changing temperatures.

*Damage from weather caused the structure to leak over time.*

# Dome Disaster

The U.S. pavilion caught fire nine years later while crews were trying to fix the leaks. The material used for the outer covering caught fire and quickly burned away. The frame still stands today and is used as an environmental museum.

*How could following the steps in the Engineering Design Process have helped prevent both the leaks and the fire?*

# Try It Yourself!

Geodesic domes are strong structures because they are built using triangles. It is very difficult to bend, twist, or collapse a triangle. Try building your own geodesic dome and test its strength.

**You will need:**

25 toothpicks
11 small balls of play dough

## Instructions:

1. Connect five toothpicks with five play-dough balls in a ring shape. This is the base for your dome.
2. Poke one toothpick into one of the balls on the base so it is pointing upward. Do the same in the ball next to it. Then connect the two toothpicks at the top using another play-dough ball. You should have formed a triangle. Continue making triangles around the base until you have formed five triangles.
3. Poke toothpicks into the sides of the top balls, forming another five-sided ring.
4. Push one upright toothpick into each top ball. Gather the ends of the five toothpicks and push them all into one final play-dough ball at the top.

Try adding weight to your dome, such as heavy envelopes. Are you surprised at how strong your dome is?

Now, try building another dome using squares on top of the base instead of triangles. Can this dome hold as much weight?

## Did you know?

Domes have been used in engineering for thousands of years. However, geodesic domes are the only kind of domes built with triangles.

# Avoiding Dome Disasters

It is important to follow the steps in the Engineering Design Process to avoid disasters. It is just as important to check domes regularly after they have been built. One broken triangle can weaken a structure. If it is not repaired, the dome can leak and even collapse. An engineer solves problems, but also tries to prevent them!

*This research station in the Antarctic lasted in the harsh climate for 35 years. Regular checks and maintenance on this dome made it last 20 years longer than expected.*

# Learning More

## Books

*Engineering Close-up* series. Crabtree Publishing Company, 2014.

Richards, Julie. *Stadiums and Domes*. Smart Apple Media, 2004.

Vorderman, Carol. *How to Be an Engineer*. DK Children, 2018.

## Websites

Learn about geodesic domes as well as other types of domes at: **www.pbs.org/wgbh/ buildingbig/dome/basics.html**

Learn more about the history of geodesic domes at: **https://kids.kiddle.co/ Geodesic_dome**

For fun engineering challenges, activities, and more, enter the code at the Crabtree Plus website below.

www.crabtreeplus.com/be-an-engineer

Your code is:
**bae04**

# Glossary

**Note: Some boldfaced words are defined where they appear in the book.**

**3-D** (THREE-DEE) *adjective*
Short for three-dimensional, an object that has length, width, and height

**earthquake** (URTH-kweyk) *noun*
A series of vibrations that begin in Earth's crust

**effective** (ih-FEK-tiv) *adjective*
Producing the correct result

**environment** (en-VAHY-ern-muh-nt) *noun* The natural surroundings of things

**frame** (freym) *noun* The structure inside a thing that holds it up

**hurricane** (HUR-i-keyn) *noun*
A severe storm with strong winds that starts over water

**model** (MOD-l) *noun*
A representation of a real object

**pavilion** (puh-VIL-yuhn) *noun* A building or large shelter used for a specific purpose

**plywood** (PLAHY-wood) *noun* A building material made up of thin layers of wood glued together

**pollute** (puh-LOOT) *verb* To make unclean

**representation** (rep-ri-zen-TEY-shun) *noun* Something that stands in place for something else

**retractable** (ri-TRAKT-abl) *adjective*
Able to be drawn back in

**shingle** (SHING-guh-l) *noun*
A thin piece of material laid in overlapping rows to cover a roof

**sphere** (sfeer) *noun*
A 3-D object that is round like a ball

**tornado** (tawr-NEY-doh) *noun*
A destructive windstorm on land that contains a long funnel-shaped cloud

*A noun is a person, place, or thing.
An adjective is a word that tells you what something is like.
A verb is an action word that tells you what someone or something does.*

# Index